BLAST OFF!
MARS

Helen and David Orm

D0543338

Copyright © ticktock Entertainment Ltd 2007
First published in Great Britain in 2006 by ticktock Media Ltd.,
Unit 2, Orchard Business Centre, North Farm Road,
Tunbridge Wells, Kent, TN2 3XF

ticktock project editor: Julia Adams
ticktock project designer: Emma Randall

We would like to thank: Sandra Voss, Tim Bones, James Powell,
Indexing Specialists (UK) Ltd.

ISBN 978 1 84696 051 2
Printed in China
A CIP catalogue record for this book is available from the British Library.
Picture credits
t=top, b=bottom, c=centre, l-left, r=right
Bridgeman Art Library:15c; ESA: 13tr, 17bl; NASA: front cover, 1tl, 1br, 6br, 7t, 7cl, 7b, 9tl, 9tr, 9c, 11tl, 11cr, 11bl, 12cl, 13bl,
17tr, 19tr, 19bl, 19br, 20tl, 20tr, 20bl, 20br, 21cl, 21tr, 21bl, 22c; NASA, James Bell, Michael Wolff, The Hubble Heritage Team:
9bl; Science Photo Library: 4/5bg (original), 12tl, 18tr, 23tr, 23bl; Shutterstock: 2/3bg, 6bl, 18bl, 24bg; ticktock picture archive: 5tl,
6/7bg, 7cr, 8bl, 8cr, 8br,10tr, 10bg, 10bl, 12b, 14tl, 14tr, 14/15bg, 16cl, 18/19bg, 19tl, 22/23bg
Every effort has been made to trace the copyright holders, and we apologise in advance for any unintentional omissions.
We would be pleased to insert the appropriate acknowledgements in any subsequent edition of this publication.

Contents

Where is Mars?

There are eight planets in our **solar system**. The planets travel around the Sun. Mars is the closest planet to Earth.

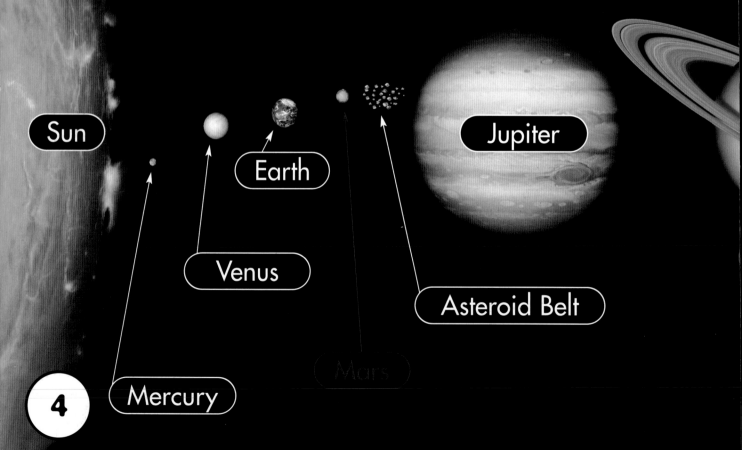

Sun

Mercury

Venus

Earth

Asteroid Belt

Mars

Jupiter

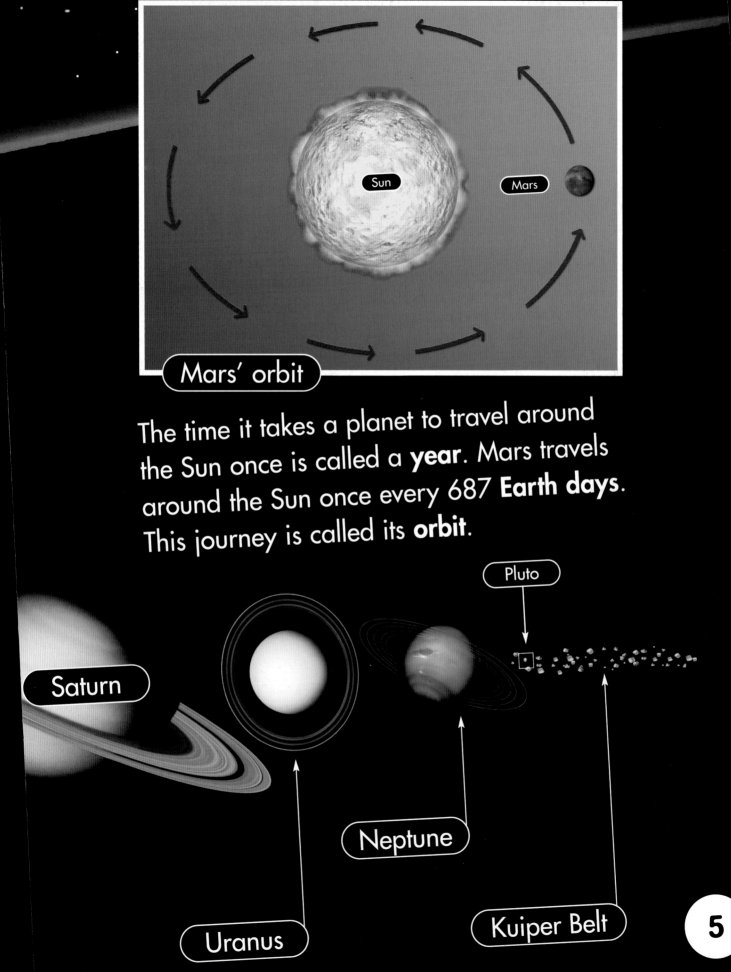

Mars' orbit

The time it takes a planet to travel around the Sun once is called a **year**. Mars travels around the Sun once every 687 **Earth days**. This journey is called its **orbit**.

Sun

Mars

Pluto

Saturn

Uranus

Neptune

Kuiper Belt

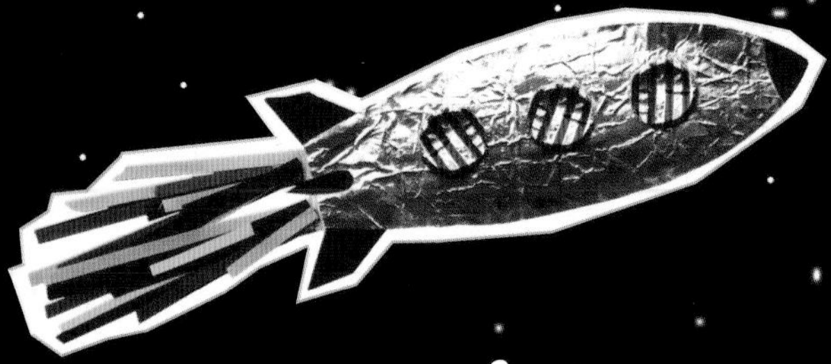

Planet Facts

The surface of Mars is dry with dusty soil. There is **iron** in the soil. The iron makes the soil red. Mars is sometimes called the 'Red Planet'.

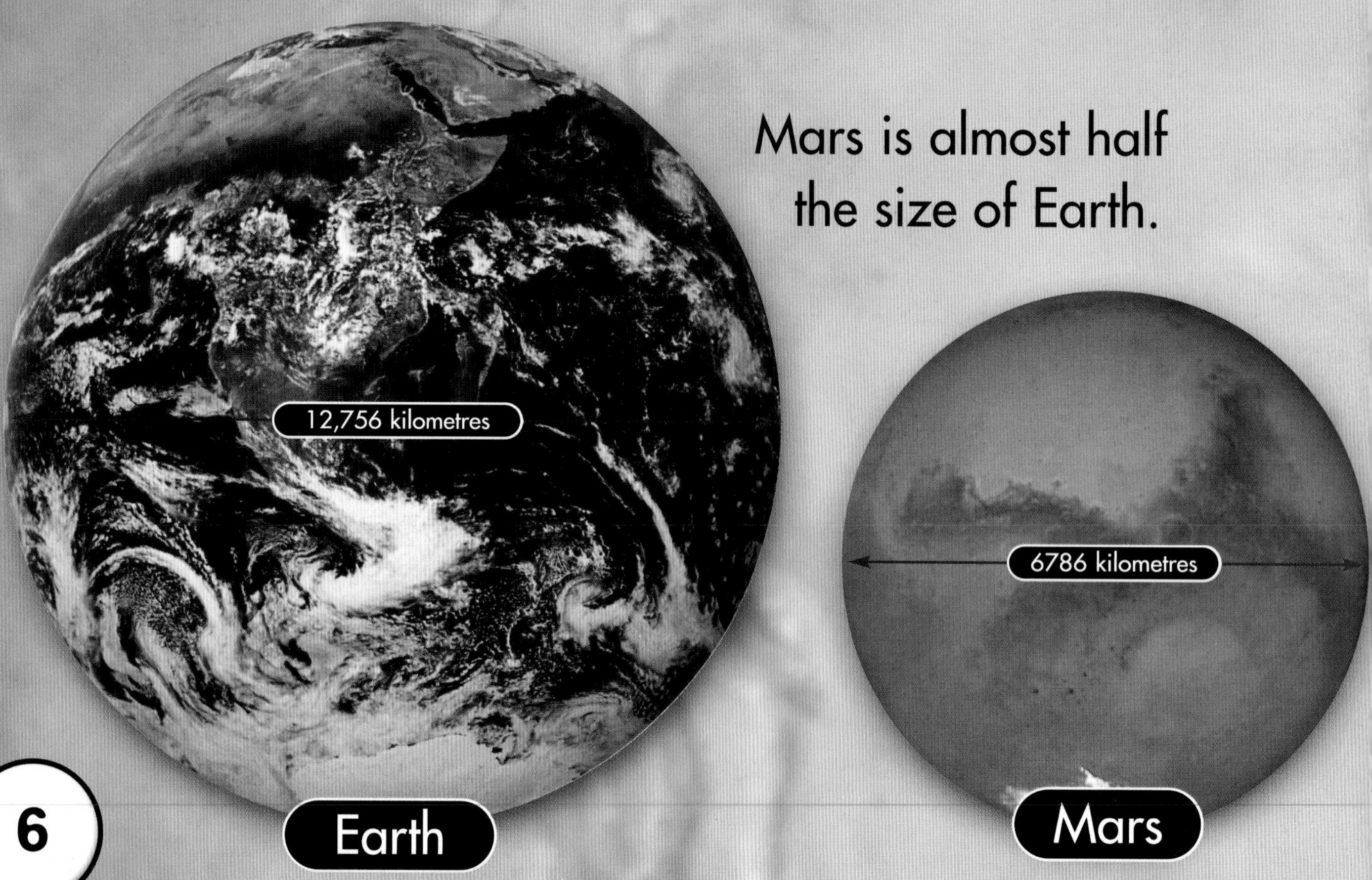

Mars is almost half the size of Earth.

12,756 kilometres

6786 kilometres

Earth

Mars

Planets are always spinning. The time a planet takes to spin around once is called a day. A day on Mars is just 41 minutes longer than an **Earth day**!

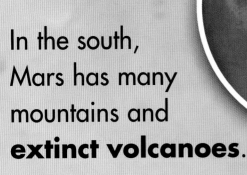

In the south, Mars has many mountains and **extinct volcanoes**.

In the north, the surface of Mars is flatter, with huge dusty plains.

Mars has a very thin **atmosphere**. It is mostly made of **carbon dioxide**. This atmosphere allows sunlight to easily reach Mars' surface during the day. But at night Mars is very cold.

During the day, the surface of Mars heats up.

At night, the thin atmosphere allows all the heat to escape.

20°C
10°C
0°C
10°C
-20°C
-30°C
-40°C
-50°C
-60°C
-70°C
-80°C
-100°C
-110°C
-120°C
-130°C
-140°C
-150°C

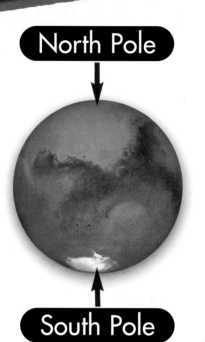

South Pole

Mars has ice at its North and South Poles. The ice is made of frozen carbon dioxide. In the summer, the ice melts. In the winter, it freezes over again.

This is the North Pole of Mars in the winter...

...and in the summer. Almost all the ice has melted.

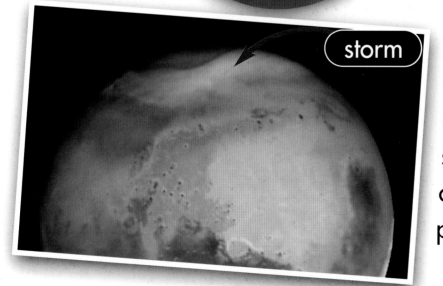

storm

Mars is very windy. Sometimes great dust storms reach speeds of up to 362 km per hour!

The Moons of Mars

Mars has two moons called Phobos and Deimos. They both **orbit** Mars.

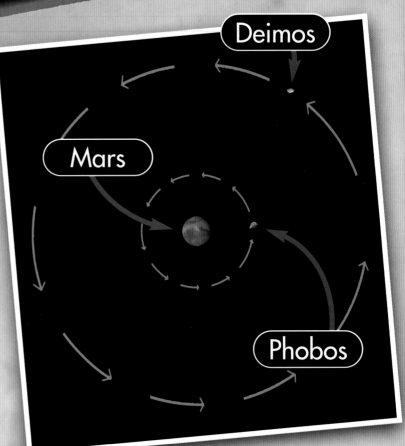

Deimos

Mars

Phobos

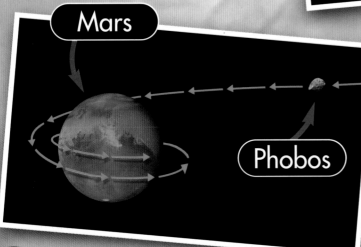

Mars

Phobos

Scientists think Phobos and Deimos used to be **asteroids**. They were flying through space. As they passed by Mars, they were pulled into orbit around the planet.

Phobos and Deimos are much smaller
than the Earth's moon

Earth's Moon

Phobos

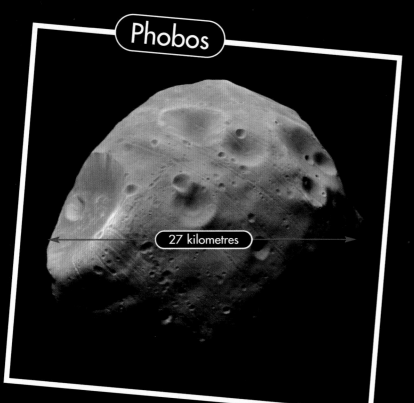

27 kilometres

3476 kilometres

Phobos is the
bigger of the two moons.
It is almost 27 km across.

Deimos

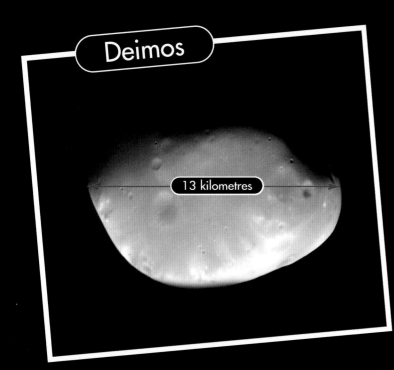

13 kilometres

Deimos is
even smaller
than Phobos.
It is about 13 km
across!

11

On the Surface

Mars has many different mountains, **craters** and **canyons**. It has the highest mountain and the largest canyon area in our **solar system**!

Olympus Mons

Olympus Mons is the highest mountain in the solar system! It is 24 km high. Mount Everest is the highest mountain on Earth.

Olympus Mons

24 kilometres

Mt Everest

8,850 m

Olympus Mons is a **volcano**, but it is not **active** anymore.

The Valles Marineris is a 4000-km-long canyon. It is nearly 11 km deep. That's about seven times deeper than the Grand Canyon on Earth! It is the largest canyon area in the solar system.

Syrtis Major is an area of dark ground on Mars' surface. It was discovered by the Dutch astronomer Christiaan Huygens. Some scientists used to think it was a huge sea.

Syrtis Major was the first area on a planet that scientists studied from Earth. They discovered it about 300 years ago using one of the first telescopes made.

Mars in History

People have always seen and known about Mars because it is a very bright object in the night sky.

Moon

Mars

This is a statue of Mars, the Roman god of war. In ancient Rome, people believed that red was a symbol for war. That is why they named the planet after this god.

This is a globe of Mars. It was made by the American scientist Percival Lowell in 1903.

Lowell thought he had discovered oceans and water canals made by Martians (beings from Mars).

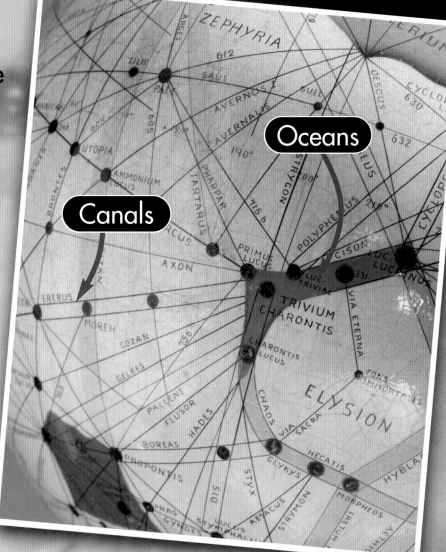

Oceans

Canals

In 1965, the **space probe** Mariner 4 took pictures of the surface of Mars. They showed that Lowell had only seen **craters** and shadows on Mars' surface.

Living on Mars

For hundreds of years, people thought that space creatures may live on Mars.

People wrote stories about Martians and other space creatures coming to Earth from Mars!

But life is only possible where there is **liquid** water. Scientists always look for signs of water when they study planets.

Some **astronomers** think these channels show there was once water on Mars. They believe these areas may be dried up rivers. If Mars had rivers, then it may also have been home to living things millions of years ago.

channel

frozen carbon dioxide on Mars

Space probes to Mars can only find frozen **carbon dioxide**. So Scientists believe that Mars is too cold for **liquid** water and life.

What Can We See?

Mars looks like a bright star from Earth. It is easy to see on clear nights. Sometimes you can even see its reddish colour.

With binoculars or a small telescope, you can see Mars as a round disc.

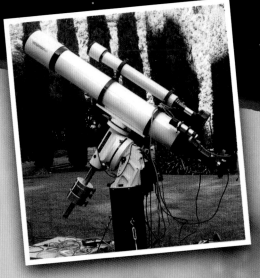

With a bigger
telescope,
you can see
some of the details of the surface
of Mars. It is possible to see if it is
summer or winter on the planet.

This huge area
of ice means it is
winter on Mars.

The Hubble Space Telescope
is out in space. It is in **orbit**
around the Earth.

Hubble sends pictures
to Earth that are really
clear, like this one.

Missions to Mars

There have been many missions to Mars. The first successful one was in 1965. It was a **space probe** called Mariner 4.

Mariner 4 took the first close-up pictures of Mars.

In July 1979, the Viking 1 lander became the first space probe to land on Mars. It took many pictures of Mars' surface.

Pathfinder rocket

Pathfinder rocket

In 1997, Mars Pathfinder rocket took a robot vehicle to Mars. The robot took pictures and tested rocks to help scientists learn about the surface of Mars.

In 2004, the Rover mission took two robots to Mars. These robots are still on the planet. They are looking for signs of **liquid** water on the surface.

Rover Robot

21

First People on Mars

Astronauts have never been to the surface of Mars. But they may be able to in the future.

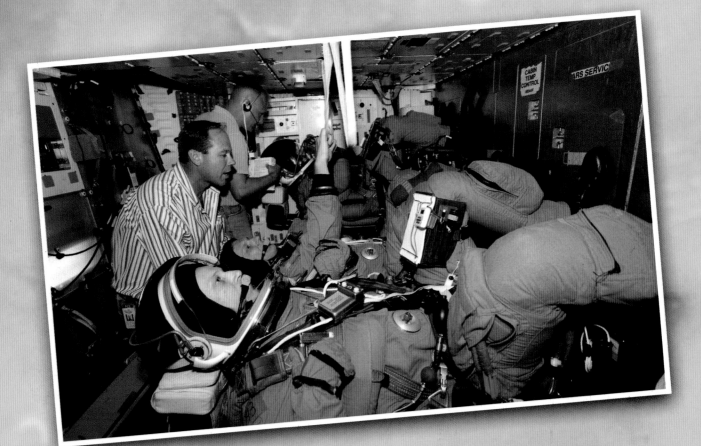

Astronauts will have to prepare very well for a journey to Mars. Flying to Mars will take nine months. It will be a tough mission.

Some scientists say it is possible to make a thicker **atmosphere** for Mars. It would take hundreds of years to do this. If it works, people could live in stations on Mars. They would have to wear space suits outside.

Then, scientists would have to change the air on Mars. This is so people could breathe the air and live without space suits. This could take 10,000 to 100,000 years.

If it works, people could move to Mars one day!

Glossary

Active volcano A volcano that is still erupting.

Asteroids Rocky objects that orbit the Sun. Most asteroids orbit the Sun between Mars and Jupiter.

Astronauts People trained to travel or work in space.

Astronomer A person who studies space, often using telescopes.

Atmosphere The gases that surround a star, planet or moon.

Canyons Long, deep river valleys.

Carbon dioxide A gas that is made when something burns.

Craters Holes in the surface of a planet made either by a volcano or when the planet is hit by a rock from space.

Earth days A day is the time it takes a planet to spin around once. A day on Earth is 24 hours long.

Extinct volcano A volcano that is no longer erupting and is not likely to do so in future.

Iron One of the heaviest metals.

Liquid Something that flows easily.

Orbit The path that a planet or other object takes round the Sun, or a satellite takes round a planet.

Solar system The Sun and everything that is in orbit around it.

Space probe A spacecraft sent from Earth to explore the solar system.

Volcano A mountain where the hot, liquid inside of a planet bursts to the surface.

Year The time it takes a planet to orbit the Sun once.

Index